Who is God?

CAROLYN NYSTROM

Illustrated by
Wayne A. Hanna

MOODY PRESS
CHICAGO

For Craig,
my small boy with
big questions

© 1980, by
THE MOODY BIBLE INSTITUTE
OF CHICAGO

ISBN: 0-8024-5992-7

Printed in the United States of America

Moody Press, a ministry of the Moody Bible Institute,
is designed for education, evangelization, and
edification. If we may assist you in knowing more about
Christ and the Christian life, please write us without
obligation: Moody Press, c/o MLM, Chicago, Illinois 60610.

Who is God? I think and think but mostly
I think of questions, because God is not
like anyone or anything that I know.

—Can God see in the dark?

—Can God hear me pray if someone else talks to Him at the same time?

—Will God hurt me?

—Does God wear clothes?

—Does God love me?

—Can I love God and fear Him too?

—How can I hear God talk?

—What does God look like?

—Did God make my toys?

—Where does God live?

—Does God know what I think?

—Does God speak English? or Spanish?

I know my grandma because I hear her voice on the phone. I know this caterpillar because I feel him walk down my finger. I know my mom because she hugs me and reads me stories—and besides, she looks different from other mothers.

But how can I know God? I have never seen Him or touched Him, and I never heard Him speak.

God is so wise and so wonderful that we cannot know everything about Him. Our minds are not strong enough. But God wants us to know some things about Himself. So He chose certain people to write a book about Him. It is called the Bible.

Everyone in my family looks different.
My sister Suzy has red hair. My daddy has a
beard. My baby brother has a fat tummy.
And my mom looks most like herself when
sitting cross-legged on the floor.
   What does God look like?

John 1:18; 4:24

The Bible says that no one has seen God because God is a spirit. That means He doesn't have a body at all. God simply doesn't "look like." But we can know what kind of person God is because for a while Jesus, God's Son, was a man. Then He had a body like ours.

But Jesus is God, and He prayed to His Father to give the Holy Spirit. That makes three. How can God be three persons and only one God?

That is a mystery called the Trinity— one of the things our minds can't totally understand about God.

A yardstick has a beginning and an end. It measures how tall I am. I begin at my feet and I end at my head. My life begins and ends too. I was born as a baby, I will live for a while, then I will die. Everyone does.

Does God?

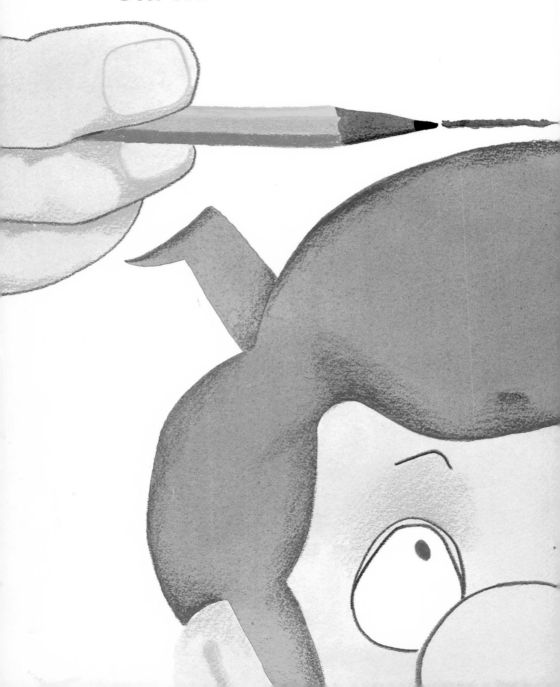

No. God is the only person who never began and never will end. God is. He always was and always will be. Not only that, God never changes. He never has and He never will.

I don't know anyone else who doesn't change at all—at least sometime.

I am learning to read. But my daddy knows more than I do. He teaches college students. Sometimes he studies books. He says the writers of those books know more than he does. And I suppose someone else taught the writers. How much does God know?

God knows all things. God never needed to learn because He knew it all in the beginning. Even the smartest person in the world does not know as much as God.

Once my mom was feeding my baby brother. But I wanted her to fix my truck right away. So I yelled, "Mom, come help me now."

Mom kept right on feeding my brother. She said, "Jimmy, I can't be in more than one place at a time."

Can God?

Psalm 139:7-12

God is everywhere—all the time. He doesn't have to fly fast from one place to another. He just *always is everywhere.* No matter where we are, God is with us.

I like that.

What is the most powerful thing in the world? I asked a lot of people. Is it a lion? Is it a king? Is it a huge coal-mining machine? Is it a bomb?

Is God more powerful than these?

God is more powerful than anything or anyone. He can do anything He chooses. God made the sky and the stars—even those we can't see. He made the whole world and everything in it. Then He called it all good. But God didn't go away. God still takes care of everything that He made— even us.

Did God make my truck?
No, but God created people and made them able to make my truck.

Some days I wake up and say to myself, "Today I'm going to be good all day. I'm going to help mother with the baby, I'm going to stay out of fights, and I'm not going to say even one naughty word."

But I always forget by supper. I'm just not perfect. Is anyone? Is God?

Psalm 18:30; Isaiah 6:1-5

God is not only perfect, He is more than perfect. He is holy. God has never done wrong. He has never made a mistake. Even His plans are perfect. Because God is perfect in every way, we can't quite imagine Him. He is so different from us. But God wants us to try to be like Him—as much as we are able. This pleases Him.

I like things fair. If Suzy gets a popsicle, I want one too. I get angry if a friend rides my bike without asking, or if someone at school grabs a book that I saw first. A grown-up usually straightens this out, but sometimes what she decides doesn't seem quite right. Is God always fair?

Deuteronomy 32:4; Romans 14:10-12

Because God is perfect in every other way, God is also perfectly fair. The Bible says that someday God will judge the whole world —every person who has ever lived.

I'm glad I'll have a fair judge. I know God won't make any mistakes.

Everyone I know gets angry. Suzy gets mad if I sneak up and pull her hair, even if I'm just playing. Mom doesn't like it if I'm late for breakfast. My teacher gets angry if I talk while she is talking. Is God ever angry?

Proverbs 6:16-19, Matthew 22:37-40; Romans 3:23; 1 John 1:9

Because God is holy, He hates all sin.
God does not want us to do anything that
shows we do not love Him or that hurts
another person. And God must punish sin.
But God wants us to tell Him we are
sorry when we do wrong. Then He will forgive
us and help us do right next time.

My daddy is in charge of my family. He works so that we can have food and a house and toys. He and Mom decide when I will go to school and where we will go to church and whether we will buy a new car. They take care of me. But I have to do what they say. If I don't, there is fast trouble. Being in charge of a family is a big job. Is anyone in charge of the whole world?

1 Chronicles 29:11-13; Psalm 8:3; Matthew 10:29

God is. Because God created the world and the heavens and the stars and the planets, God can be in charge of them too. The Bible says He holds the stars in place but He cares even when a sparrow falls to the ground. God is in charge of people too—each of us.

I'm glad God is so wise and strong and holy. I wouldn't want anyone less than God to have that kind of control.

I know lots of nice people. But none of them is good all the time. Even my best friend lied when he said he didn't have my red crayon. Later, I saw him using it, and I knew that crayon was mine. Is God like that?

Psalm 100:5

No, God is good all the way through.

When I think of all these truths about God, I can almost feel my head stretching. But the Bible says something else about God. It says God loves His people. He calls them "friends."

Exodus 15:11-13

So I worship God. I say, "God, You are wonderful. Thank You for letting me know You. I love You."

God loves me too.
He is my friend.